Castara Colouring Book

It is well documented that, for many people (adults and children alike), colouring is a therapeutic, stress-relieving pastime.

What could be better, then, than colouring pictures of beautiful Castara? While away the hours dreaming of being (back) in Tobago, sunning yourself on the fine golden sand, bathing and snorkelling in the crystal clear blue Caribbean Sea, or enjoying a rum punch as the sun goes down.

If you have visited before, within these pages you will find familiar scenes and people waiting to welcome you back. If you haven't been here yet, these pictures are designed to encourage you to get on that flight to sunny Tobago!

Unlike most other colouring books which are usually filled with whimsical and cartoon images, mine are full of real pictures.

In this case, the colouring pages were created from photographs I took during our first four-month stay in Castara. We spent our time getting to know the people and learning about Tobago's rich history and culture. Within this book, you will find images of the businesses in Castara as well as views of Big Bay and Little Bay. Look out for pictures of the traditional clay oven where Mrs Taylor and Daddy Ben bake the most delicious loaves and fruit buns. There are drawings here to inspire you and get your creative juices flowing!!

Grab your favourite pens or pencils and let your imagination and creativity run riot. I use high quality fine-tip felt pens for the details, and coloured pencils for the larger areas, but the choice is yours. Some people like to put a water colour wash across the whole picture before they begin. It's your creation. It's up to you!

Cut out your finished work and display it somewhere as in inspiration to travel further for longer, or as a reminder of places you've already been to.

Keep in touch with me at Happy Days Travel Blog or on social media:

@happydaystravelblog   @happydayswriter

Show me your creations, follow my travels, and tell me about yours!

Copyright © 2019 Happy Days Publishing - All Rights Reserved. Further information from https://happydaystravelblog.com

CASTARA GOVERNMENT PRIMARY SCHOOL

ANYTHING IS WORTH DOING IS WORTH DOING WELL

www.ingramcontent.com/pod-product-compliance
Lightning Source LLC
Chambersburg PA
CBHW080904220526
45466CB00011BA/3458